AFTER

poems by

Babo Kamel

Finishing Line Press
Georgetown, Kentucky

AFTER

Copyright © 2018 by Babo Kamel
ISBN 978-1-63534-584-1 First Edition
All rights reserved under International and Pan-American Copyright Conventions. No part of this book may be reproduced in any manner whatsoever without written permission from the publisher, except in the case of brief quotations embodied in critical articles and reviews.

ACKNOWLEDGMENTS

With appreciation to the editors who first published these poems, often in different versions
2 River View: "Not knowing he's dead";
Mizmor L'David Anthology: "Statue: Mother and Child";
San Pedro River Review: "What She Cannot Tell";
Rat's Ass Review: "On Monday";
Mobius: The Journal of Social Change: "Please Find Us";
2 River View: "What began with Chagall";
Redactions: Poetry & Poetics: "Wedding Song";
Marblehead Magazine: "Blue Circus";
Bracken Magazine: "Revenant";
Verdad: "And when you look into the eye of the horse."

Publisher: Leah Maines
Editor: Christen Kincaid
Cover Art: Norman Leibovitch http://www.normanleibovitch.com/
Author Photo: Orin Edwards
Cover Design: Elizabeth Maines McCleavy

Printed in the USA on acid-free paper.
Order online: www.finishinglinepress.com
also available on amazon.com

Author inquiries and mail orders:
Finishing Line Press
P. O. Box 1626
Georgetown, Kentucky 40324
U. S. A.

Table of Contents

Not knowing he's dead 1

Statue: Mother and Child 2

The Photograph 3

The Photograph Responds 4

What Remains 5

What She Cannot Tell 6

On Monday 7

Please Find Us 8

The Painter over Vitebsk 9

Which way, which way to play this violin 10

What began with Chagall 11

Wedding Song 12

After the Wedding 13

The painter changes his palette 14

The Painter at his Easel 15

Blue Circus 16

Revenant 17

And when you look into the eye of the horse 18

After Reading You I Dream in Chagall 19

For my parents

Not knowing he's dead

after Chagall

my father dreams life around him. Lovers next door
sigh through tangles of stars, berate the stun of dawn

A man delivers milk like morning news in bottles
cream rising reminds him of headlines,
one war ending, another about to begin

In the schoolyard down the street, children
chase each other into their futures
The girl in the pink jacket will not return on Monday

After last night's rain, autumn leaves fall into red and yellow
abandonments, collage like random footprints
leading there, and there and there

Evening and the dream tires of itself, rolls over
decides what color to follow
My father calls to it as if it were a lost dog

leans against a long-gone wall, an empty red leash in his hand

Statue: Mother and Child

after Bezalel Malchi's sculpture

Dumb eyed, refusing light, like one awakened from dreaming
loved ones back again, the bronze woman of my childhood

comes knocking. I remember her on the library stairs half-
shadowed, behind blue rope, barring entrance to the second story

the way memory lets you go only so far, the rest a fiction
you cling to, the way that mother still clings to the babe

in her arms, somewhere, somewhere,
somewhere in Montreal she must be

covered with cloth, and decades of dust
archived with records, microfiche, photographs

a thing long forgotten and un-yearned for
And so she knocks and becomes every refugee

throat dry, surrounded by sand, sea or snow
arms around a child, like a womb on the outside

and everywhere walls. Walls of steerage
My grandmother, aged 17, sails into a language

unknown, home an idea wrapped in a Russian shawl
and the word pogrom, repeating itself

like a tattoo on her tongue
Her name was Fanny

She read Anna Karenina in Yiddish
She never went back

The Photograph

after Roman Vishniac

It's 1939 and he still lives
in Kazimierz. In the bakery doorway
he stares down late afternoon
that slips into its cloak
of shadows. You could call him
Yacov, Hershel or any of the other boys
forced to march out of their names

But he still stands, although his heart
must adopt the rhythm of sparrows
One hand curves against his side
as if he holds a stone, but there is no stone
only a dusting of flour, leftover from Challahs
braided between cracks of dawn

We don't know what he risked to do this
How he left dream-soaked nights
for streets bound to spit him out to ghettos
across the river. We do know this:
Someone must make the bread. Even in war
To feed the living

The Photograph Responds

Just a few breads left
You take a photo of me
in Kazimierz. A moment caught
like a fish from the river. But you cannot
eat a moment

                It swims away

Takes a piece of us as it goes

In Kazimierz, we try to be invisible
so we will not disappear
the children
                learn to whisper

Your camera cannot steal
my soul. It's already gone
into hiding. Or maybe it left on a train

To steal a soul, you must chew on its music
take your time and swallow every note,
plunder its heart until it forgets its rhythm

You must first learn its shape
when it breathes fully. You must study
how it leans softly on another
or how it lifts itself to mingle with the rain

You must become that breath and take it away
You must become that other and take it away
You must become the rain and take it away

You must understand what will drop it to its knees
But leave it a last bit of hope, let that hope linger

then take that away too

What Remains

after Roman Vishniac

Had the photo not been in black and white
had the woman's shawl been more than its remains
had her eyes allowed light to find them
had the face of the young boy not begun to age
out of the moment out of the moment out of the moment
had even the rotting fruit in the cart not seemed so wanted
had it not rained all morning
had the horses not stood, muddy hooved on damp stones
had the damp stones not lay like freshly caught fish, their fight over
had the men on the corner not stood black coated and hunched
as if they were a minyan devoid of prayer
had the gas lamps been lit, instead of standing already forgetting
had the three-story buildings at the end of the street
not appeared to be fading out of their outlines
had the photographer not been here
we would not see the three-year-old girl
rain boots unbuckled, head tilted
with a hand in her pocket, as if she held a bright red apple there

What She Cannot Tell

after Chagall's The Three Candles

That she saw the bride dance with her lover in the sky.
That the sky drank the bride's bouquet of lily and gardenia.

That three white candles, taller than rooftops, stood guard melting.
That angels felt hot wax on their wings and tumbled into sound.

That sound was a man playing a violin tune he had not yet written.
That as he played he rose up past the angels tumbling.

That the harlequin stood stranded on the fence below.
That he begged his yellow clarinet for a note that could remember.

That the villagers swept dust from their doorways.
That children rolled walnuts into holes they dug.

That the blue donkey in the corner knew only his bucket.
That the bucket was filled with water and the water was sweet.

That she was just a distant child, hardly visible in the painting.
That she believed two souls could truly come together.

That there was nothing crystal about that night.
That the concussion of broken glass had not yet reached them.

On Monday

> *after Chagall's* Phaeton

A thunder of orange, brash against the sky
then flash after flash like a migraine

We stood stunned as statues or dolls
in flames. This was our village

We knew our names and the smell of earth
where we planted our dead. We made sure

that even the young knew what the days wanted
Until that morning the stranger soared

above the roofs, riding his chariot fast and hard
like a high-jacked birthright, flirting with the sun

until metal began to melt. And we stood
Stood in front of our doors and watched it all

as if a godless thing had fallen, burning into the dazzle of himself
to leave behind as souvenirs, the singed wings of horses

Please Find Us

> *"no one leaves home unless*
> *home is the mouth of a shark"*
> Warshan Shire

We remember each detail. The hallway, lightless. How the floor rebelled
The tiny room at the end, claustrophobic with its pink everything. The story
of breadcrumbs, how birds ate the way home
.
When the fires come we take what we can—
candles, blankets, one small doll
But we leave ourselves behind
in the dust under the bed, even as it blazes
and in the small corner where the cat sleeps
we leave a hairbrush

We hide anywhere we can—
cornfields, alleys, that one long night
we slip into, as if it is a flowing robe
In its sleeves we leave fragments of prayers
in its pocket, a tooth wrapped in cloth

No map for this. The geography is too cruel
mountains have no footholds
the ocean bullies us, finds each hole in our boat
we scale a wall, and then another appears
we have never seen so many backs

The Painter over Vitebsk

after Chagall

Over there in crimson sky, a Palomino
airborne through amber. Oh, what delight
to sit rooftop, enticing moon
to rise against its nature. Night's lyric
undresses in full daylight, where we roam un-asleep
in the grand gaudy business of dreams

Call the lovers to float again, as once they did
when each sweet touch left its knowing on the skin
See them a waltz above the huddled
houses whispering to each other

Tell the circus boy on the red pony his childhood
is the dove resting on his shoulder—
the closest he will come to wings of his own
And that sometimes, memory is the weight of what is lost

And while the church in the distance winks at god
a woman holding a child like a puppet makes her way
out of the painting. She doesn't see the giant bouquet
of dahlia and trumpet vine. Or the revolution of colors
beneath the grey pavement. She knows only this:
she must keep moving out of what feels like madness

If you should see her, years from now
in this painted moment, framed
hanging on a wall in Saint Paul de Vence
tell her I meant no harm. That she and the child survived
That the war is over

Which way, which way to play this violin

after Chagall's Composition, 1976

to yesterday's little green goat in the yard,
the tin bell around her neck, that sweet sound of morning
waking the whole village from its blue reverie? The simple
relief of gathering eggs, straw clinging to shoes
and the wall around town laughing at itself

Everything knew what to do. The moon
did not outstay its welcome. The insomniac
put down her pen. And in the gardens
unpicked bouquets of hollyhock and foxglove
delighted in being overlooked

The dark- eyed stray that was everyone's pet
had a different name at each doorway
and each name was a story, and each was true

And when the dog, full of his names
was no longer hungry, he would lie down under a birch tree
hind leg twitching, dreaming himself

into a poem, being written now. At 3 AM. A night without stars.   A
bomb goes off

       in Brussels,   but
we   can't hear   it yet. A bomb went off
           in Baghdad   but we
can't   hear   it   yet. A bomb
       went off   in Suruc but we   can't
hear   it yet   A bomb
     goes off in Potiksum   but we can't hear

it   yet   a bomb   goes off   but we can't hear it

yet
    this night without stars remembers a man

who plays a violin in a painting. And the man calls to the music.
And the music not knowing its name, is always hungry

What Began with Chagall

They were out of place, this explosion of roses in the swirl of blue town
The neighbors awoke not to the gentle sun
but to the grin of crimson

The roses were all wrong, blooms as huge as impossible promises
but they were loud and brash and totally in love
with themselves

Folks on one side of the street kept their distance
gathered blue paint in the fields. Those on the other side
knelt before the roses, learning the language

On Tuesday, the roses blast open
a shrapnel of petals landed on roofs and roads
Landed on the faces of the town folks

At first the children ran around trying to catch the petals on their tongues
Church bells were silenced, suffocating in petals

By Wednesday, some neighbors were begging for blue
to pull the red thorns from their skin

Wedding Song

after Chagall's Les Amoureux Dans Le Bouquet de Fleurs

He hid me in lilacs. He wanted me a bride forever
He said the crystals on my gown seemed stars had broken
and found a home there. They were only cut glass
but a man needs his dreams and his visions

He kept painting me over and over. I floated above our village
sideways and upside down, oh how he tried to keep me
from gravity. Sometimes I rode on a rooster
so red, its feathers seemed dipped in sunsets

Once I was swept up in the unblinking eye of a cloud
But I could still hear the clown play a purple clarinet
and the bells from the green roofed church
that we never would enter

It went on like that for years, he was in love
with indigo, for him it held the sweet
stain of our marriage, and the sound of a blue violin
He said he opened a window and I blew in

After the Wedding

after Chagall

Asleep under the bouquet, they forgot their names.
She could taste his dreams.
He gathered his disappointments, scattered them on a hill for the sparrows.
She heard their flight. Followed them.
They flew into her mouth. She swallowed their little disasters.
At 6 AM, the news reported the theft. It fractured the morning.
Left a piece of the sun on their pillow.

The Painter Changes his Palette

after Chagall

Although I may never abandon this binge
of blue, I wanted to shake things up

let the lovers rise slowly into sunglow
years after the wedding

Never more their bodies than now
her hand rests on his pulse

She knows the loneliness
that resides there, in the moment before touch

I will let them sway there on the roof
unaware of the brown goat watching from above

or the vase filled with marigolds
taller than any tree. And I will not eavesdrop

on their sweet murmurings as the day
awakens to itself or remind them

that at night she gathers up his losses
takes them into herself, with each sleeping breath

The Painter at his Easel

after Chagall

It's not the painter at his easel
but rather a winged thing of a man

He imagines her in his orbit
Mistakes for love his blue obsession

mute to whisperings
of the swallow on his shoulder

don't oppress her with foxglove
and moons dripping dogwood

don't fill her with oils
linseed, poppyseed and walnut

Forever bridal, she looks away
from the man angel, eludes perfection

If only wings could listen

Blue Circus

after Chagall

She's lost her bouquet
before the slip
from the swing
Legs arching toward the moon,
a rouged circus prop
she weaves between shadow and light

This is purple loss. Iris or violet
given by a lover
on her ascent to the lean trapeze
She swayed above the crowds
Was it the scent of love
that threw her off

A lark
small like a child's mouth
tries to save her
reaches for her ankle
with its beak

Her hands, open as fans
reach down to the lover
the flame thrower, the hard
green back of a well-trained pony

The muffled voice of the ringmaster
finally stills
She dangles
wingless
solo
destined to feel
when the body falls
how thin air is

Revenant

She offers a palm, cradles baby carrots
Damp earth clings
to the roots. Her babushka
an ambush of roses
from the Russia
my grandmother fled—
a town I can't pronounce

It's the same each time
I can't find the car
My keys are brass knuckles
Grandmother must be waiting

My grandmother is a fish
swimming out of her own watery
heart. There/not there/there again

I take the carrots. *For the world that ended*
Take small bites. Swallow the earth

And when you look into the eye of the horse

after Chagall's I and the Village

its pupil white and transparent
and see the horse -dreams there
that the horse is dreaming of the cow
who is only a cow without dreams of her own
milk squirting into the bucket
that the girl in the green skirt leans over
careful not to waste a drop
and the girl imagines herself outside of the village
with its lifeblood of gossip and crooked capped boys,
with violets in their hearts, as if these were enough
and the cobbler's son looks into her eyes
and sees her girl -dreams there
sees them distant and strange
like paintings with perspectives flung sideways

She dreams of a soldier, in a ragged jacket
whose face inhabits the entire doorway of a church
and of a sky so tiny she could swallow it
so that entire galaxies swirl in her chest
In the red glitter of stars, she remains
bride forever and floats to a whole circus of violins
tasting of amber and rain

and she looks into the eye of the painter

and the cobbler's boy seeing this, stops breathing
for a moment, a sound is so loud that the cow
in the horse's dream looks up and
steps out of it, into something vast and blue

And the girl continues to milk the air
The bucket holds on to its emptiness

The horse can't help what it dreams

After Reading You I Dream in Chagall

for Larry Levis

I fell asleep with your book in my hands
whole universes reside between commas

And what you did with time—making it sing
endless arias in which a wasp escapes a burnt hive

or a girl in a "thin blue dress" resides forever
Lovers float in clouds to a circus of serenades,

melodies mist them with fragrances of apples
like the one cold against my cheek,

see how it leaves a red memory
on the skin. If this were a painting

it would belong in Paris with a lost umbrella
after rain has left its story

on the street named for Lorca

It must have been some kind of wonderful fever
that left you famished for a world

swollen with possibility and nothingness at the same time
the way a dead painter or poet is here and not here

finger strokes on the canvas, breath on the page
like those private hauntings, wanting to be

alone but unable to bear the burden of it, the gnaw,
the dark hallway down which we watch ourselves disappear

and call ourselves back again into the half- light of being
We open doors and windows, let in sun, that constant fellow

like an old friend we take for granted, and for a moment
we remember to celebrate the drying of dishes

a found blue glove, the spider we sweep from our doorsteps.
Night finds us dancing in our sleep to rhythms

between heartbeats, where our dead come to greet us
their bodies full, warm, breathing

We rise to meet them and are not afraid

Originally from Montreal, Canada, **Babo Kamel** now resides in Venice, Florida. She has taught writing at North Shore Community College in Lynn, Ma and to various community groups. Some of her most fulfilling work was with former gang members. Her poems have appeared in literary journals in the US, Australia, and Canada. Some of these include *Painted Bride Quarterly, Abyss & Apex, The Greensboro Review, Cleaver, The Grolier Poetry Prize, Rabbit, Contemporary Verse 2, Rust +Moth, Mobius, a Journal of Social Change, 2River Review, The San Pedro River Review, Redactions, The Inflectionist Review* and *Bracken*. She was a winner of The Charlotte Newberger Poetry Prize and is a three-time Pushcart nominee. You can find her at www.babokamel.com

www.ingramcontent.com/pod-product-compliance
Lightning Source LLC
LaVergne TN
LVHW041521070426
835507LV00012B/1730